"WHEN DID I EVER SAY I WAS A GANGSTA RAPPER? IS FRANK SINATRA A GANGSTA SINGER? IS STEVEN SEAGAL A GANGSTA ACTOR? . . . THAT'S SUCH A LIMITED TERM. . . . I'M AN ARTIST. AND I RAP ABOUT THE OPPRESSED TAKING BACK THEIR PLACE. I RAP ABOUT FIGHTING BACK. TO ME, MY LYRICS AND MY VERSES ARE ABOUT STRUGGLING AND OVERCOMING."

TUPAC SHAKUR

1971–1996

ABDO
Publishing Company

TUPAC SHAKUR

MULTI-PLATINUM RAPPER

BY ASHLEY RAE HARRIS

CREDITS

Published by ABDO Publishing Company, 8000 West 78th Street, Edina, Minnesota 55439. Copyright © 2010 by Abdo Consulting Group, Inc. International copyrights reserved in all countries. No part of this book may be reproduced in any form without written permission from the publisher. The Essential Library™ is a trademark and logo of ABDO Publishing Company.

Printed in the United States of America,
North Mankato, Minnesota
092009
112010

 PRINTED ON RECYCLED PAPER

Editor: Holly Saari
Copy Editor: Erika Wittekind
Interior Design and Production: Becky Daum
Cover Design: Becky Daum

Library of Congress Cataloging-in-Publication Data
Harris, Ashley Rae.
  Tupac Shakur : multi-platinum rapper / Ashley Rae Harris.
    p. cm. — (Lives cut short)
  Includes bibliographical references.
  ISBN 978-1-60453-791-8
  1. Shakur, Tupac, 1971-1996—Juvenile literature. 2. Rap musicians—United States—Biography—Juvenile literature. I. Title.
  ML3930.S48H37 2010
  782.421649092—dc22
  [B]
                                        2009034356

TABLE OF CONTENTS

1

TAKING THE STAGE

Tupac Shakur was 18 years old when he stood onstage, looking out at the crowd at the Marin City Festival in California in 1989. It was a very important day: he finally had the chance to rap in front of a real audience. This was big—bigger than rapping with his buddies in the streets or performing in the auditorium of his old high school. This was not just about entertaining. This was a chance to share his ideas about the world, about being African-American, and about growing up poor and living in the ghetto.

▶ TUPAC SMILES BEFORE A STAGE PERFORMANCE.

This performance would be for the most important people in his life: his mother, who was recovering from a drug addiction, and his aunt Gloria, who had been there for him since he was a little boy. It also would be for his stepfather, Mutulu, who would not be at the performance because he was in jail. It would be for his friends who had died by gunshot in Baltimore. It would be for the thugs and the hustlers, the single mothers, and the street kids. It would be for the struggle.

Marin City, California

When Tupac first moved to California, he lived in Marin City, which is primarily composed of African Americans. It is a poor city surrounded by wealthy, white communities.

Marin City shares a zip code with Sausalito, a primarily white city. The differences in racial demographics between the two cities have led to tension. Despite their extreme poverty, Marin City residents often do not want to work in Sausalito or other nearby towns they could get to by bus. Sausalito residents are hesitant to hire Marin City employees. Each town views the other with prejudice and suspicion based on a history of racial discrimination. In order to earn a living, some Marin City residents turn to illegal methods, including dealing drugs.

A POWERFUL PERFORMANCE

Tupac felt the surge of excitement as he took the microphone and began rapping. With beats and vocals behind him, the young man crossed the stage, waving one hand in the air to keep rhythm, while his words traveled through the crowd.

▲ TUPAC RAPPING IN FRONT OF AN ENERGETIC CROWD

His lyrics touched on the disconnect between the promise of the American dream and the reality of African-American life: "The American dream wasn't meant for me / Cuz Lady Liberty's a hypocrite, she lied to me / Promised me freedom, education, equality / Never gave nothing but slavery."[1]

The lyrics were beautiful and serious. Some people may have marveled at how this young man had gained such insight into the world's workings. He had an air of guarded confidence that developed from growing up on the streets, yet his ideas were educated and political. It was a striking contrast—one that would characterize him throughout his short life.

Onstage in Marin City that day, Tupac did not know that he would record multiple top-selling records and star in several films before meeting an early death by gunshot at age 25. He could not know he would become a worldwide idol and help re-create hip-hop in the United States. He only wanted his voice to be heard and to be able to share his message. When he completed his performance, the crowd erupted in applause.

"The Rose That Grew from Concrete"

In addition to being a rapper, Tupac was also a poet. One of his well-known poems, "The Rose That Grew from Concrete," describes a rose that has gone against nature's laws and grown where it should not have. It has been said that the poem serves as a metaphor for Tupac's own life. He was successful despite his upbringing in the ghetto—like a rose that grew from concrete.

A SHORT BUT INFLUENTIAL LIFE

In his short life, Tupac Shakur would be both highly criticized and widely esteemed. He would become an inspiring rapper, actor, poet, and activist. Yet, he would have several run-ins with the law. He would be arrested for assault, imprisoned, and targeted by critics for his offensive lyrics

▲ IN HIS SHORT LIFE, TUPAC ACCOMPLISHED MANY
THINGS, INCLUDING MAKING MUSIC ALBUMS AND ACTING
IN MOVIES.

and dangerous lifestyle. While he lived a life
of contrasts, one thing is certain: his voice was
heard.

2

GROWING UP
ON THE STREETS

upac Amaru Shakur was born as Lesane Parish Crooks on June 16, 1971, in New York City. His mother, Afeni Shakur, eventually renamed him after the revolutionary Tupac Amaru, who led an uprising against an oppressive regime in Peru. Tupac means "shining serpent, blessed one" in an Incan language, and Shakur means "thankful to God" in Arabic.

Tupac's early years were spent in the African-American community of Harlem, New York. There, he grew up among strong females. As an

▸ TUPAC GREW UP IN A GHETTO IN HARLEM, NEW YORK.

activist and a paralegal, Afeni helped many low-income New Yorkers with their legal problems. Tupac said, "My mother taught me three things: respect, knowledge, search for knowledge. It's an eternal journey."[1] His aunt Gloria Cox helped keep the family together with home-cooked meals and celebrations with his many cousins. In 1975, his half sister, Sekyiwa, was born. He later said that she developed the strength and intellect for which the females in his family were known.

AN ACTIVIST MOTHER

Tupac's mother was a member of the Black Panthers, a radical African-American liberation organization that was often targeted by police. The Black Panthers were committed to gaining freedom for African Americans and poor people, even if this meant engaging in violent acts. Afeni had grown up poor and wanted to change the current system of racial injustice. She became a leader in the organization.

Black Panthers

In 1966, law student Huey Newton and social worker Bobby Seale founded the Black Panthers in Oakland, California. The official style of the Panthers included black leather jackets and berets, and they armed themselves with guns and other weapons, which was legal at the time. The group was inspired by Malcolm X, an African-American civil rights leader who advocated fighting violence with violence. He was assassinated in 1965, although the Panthers remained a strong force until the late 1970s. The group eventually split because of internal problems, including drug use and crimes committed by its leaders.

▲ In 1969, Afeni Shakur was arrested for her criminal actions as a member of the Black Panthers.

In April 1969, when she was 21 years old and two years before Tupac was born, Afeni was arrested—along with 20 other Black Panthers—and charged with conspiracy and weapons possession. She went to jail but was released on bail in January 1970. She became pregnant with Tupac during this time. In February 1971, Afeni was put back in jail after other accused Black Panthers left town. In May, she was found not guilty on all charges. One month later, she gave birth to Tupac. He once said, "So I was cultivated in prison. My embryo was in prison."[2] Even after her release, the Federal Bureau of Investigation (FBI) kept watch on her for years.

Afeni continued with her cause. Her strong commitment took up most of her time, which disappointed Tupac. He sometimes wished they could spend more time together. Of his early childhood, he said, "I used to feel like she cared more about *the* people instead of *her* people."[3]

Afeni Shakur

Afeni's choice to join the violent Black Panthers activists made sense given her history. Growing up, she was a thoughtful and talented young woman, and she was accepted to the prestigious School of Performing Arts in New York City. Despite her success, she did not like being poorer than her classmates. She started cutting classes and eventually dropped out entirely.

After dropping out of school, Afeni became interested in African-American history and identity. She began attending political events, where she learned about the Black Panthers. The Panthers were committed to doing whatever it took in order to gain rights for African Americans and poor people. This included killing, if they thought it was necessary. The group wanted better housing, schools, and an end to police brutality. For Afeni, the rebellious, powerful message about gaining freedom from racial and class inequality and moving toward a brighter future for African Americans felt exactly right. She not only joined the group but also quickly rose to the top as an important leader of the group's New York chapter.

Still, Afeni cared deeply about her children. She desperately wanted them to grow up to be strong, independent, and smart, and she took steps to ensure their education and well-being.

FATHER FIGURES

Though the family unit was close during Tupac's early childhood, he longed for a father. Tupac's biological father was out of the picture. Reflecting on the lack of a father in his life, Tupac said, "My mother couldn't show me where my manhood was. You need a man to teach you how to be a man."[4] He believed that a father would have taught him discipline and confidence. Tupac also felt lonely at times and recalled spending long hours watching television by himself.

Despite not having a father to raise him, Tupac had a few strong male role models during childhood. Each represented different sides of who he became as an adult. Mutulu Shakur, Afeni's longtime boyfriend and Tupac's stepfather figure, was a community activist who taught Tupac karate. Legs, a gang member and a hustler, would bring Tupac's family food and money and taught Tupac street survival tips. Tupac admired him, but the relationship was limited by Legs's involvement in illegal activity:

He took care of me, gave me money, but he was like a criminal too. He was a drug dealer out there doing his thing—he only came, brought me money, and then left.[5]

His uncle Tom Cox, or T. C., who was Aunt Gloria's husband, was a family man and a hard worker. T. C. taught Tupac the importance of taking care of one's family.

LEARNING TO WORK HARD

Afeni worked hard to make sure her kids received the best education possible, both at home and at school. She spent time and money getting them admitted to the best schools available, and she was adamant that they work hard and take their education seriously. At home, she spoke to them as if they were adults and informed them about current events, politics, music, and art. She brought them to rallies to hear what African-American leaders were saying about the government, the economy, and police brutality. Regarding Tupac's education, she said, "I knew I was raising a young black man in a society that kills young black men, and that his best weapon would be a strong, brilliant, and agile mind."[6] Afeni's ideas about schooling were so strong that she used reading as a form of punishment and to

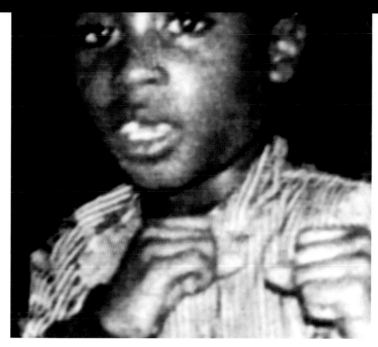

▲ IN HIS YOUTH, TUPAC EXPERIENCED BOTH CHALLENGES
AND OPPORTUNITIES.

teach her children discipline. Instead of receiving
a time-out for misbehavior, Tupac had to read
and summarize newspaper passages.

Tupac became politically conscious at
an early age. He claimed he wanted to be a
"revolutionary" when he grew up.[7] He even began
speaking at political rallies. His first public-
speaking event took place when he was just seven
years old. In front of a large group of activists,
he read aloud a poem he had written about his
godfather, Geronimo Pratt, who was a criminally
accused Black Panther.

OPPORTUNITIES

Although the family lacked money, Tupac's childhood was filled with many creative and educational opportunities. The community and family network was strong and supportive. His mother encouraged him to write and express his opinions, feelings, and ideas on paper. He loved music, including soul musician Gil Scott-Heron and rhythm and blues (R & B) star Bobby Brown. Tupac also liked acting. He often made up skits to act out with his cousins. At age 11, Tupac began acting with a theater group called the 127th Street Ensemble. When he was 12, he starred as Travis in the play *A Raisin in the Sun* and had the opportunity to perform at the Apollo Theater, a prestigious performing arts center in Harlem. Tupac also performed scenes from the play at a presidential campaign rally for candidate Jesse Jackson in 1984.

In 1982, the FBI came after the Black Panthers again, seeking Tupac's stepfather figure, Mutulu, and a group of other men for their role

Tupac's Favorite Play

One of Tupac's favorite plays was one in which he acted, *A Raisin in the Sun.* Written by Lorraine Hansberry in 1958, the play tells the story of a poor, African-American family that moves from a Chicago tenement into a white neighborhood. The play is about maintaining family pride in the face of poverty. It includes strong female characters who may resemble Tupac's own female relatives.

▲ THE INVOLVEMENT OF AFENI, *CENTER*, IN THE BLACK
PANTHERS CONTINUED TO HAUNT THE SHAKUR FAMILY.

in an armed robbery in which a guard had been
killed. Mutulu went into hiding. Tupac and
Sekyiwa feared that they were being followed by
FBI agents. Tupac later said that he believed the
FBI would always target him, as they did when
he was a child, because of his mother's association
with the Black Panthers.

In 1984, Afeni lost her job as a paralegal,
likely because of her association with Mutulu
and the Black Panthers. It was the last straw
for the Shakurs. They packed up and moved to
Baltimore, Maryland, one of the most crime-
ridden cities in the United States.

3

NEW CITY, SAME STRUGGLE

The Shakurs hoped the move to Baltimore would allow them to live in a better environment. But they ended up living in the slums in a rat-infested house with little heat. Their new city posed other problems as well. As Tupac said,

Baltimore has the highest rate of teen pregnancy, the highest rate of AIDS within the black community, the highest rate of teens killing teens, the highest rate of teen suicide, and the highest rate of blacks killing blacks . . . and this is where we chose to live.[1]

▶ THE SHAKURS MOVED INTO A TENEMENT IN BALTIMORE.

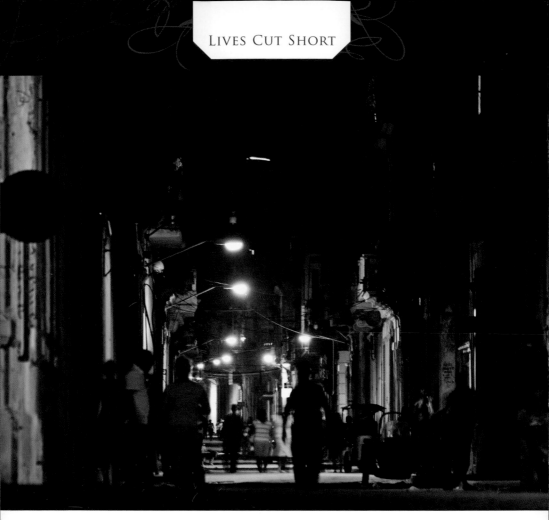

▲ IN BALTIMORE, TUPAC ENCOUNTERED AN
ENVIRONMENT SIMILAR TO THE GHETTOS OF NEW YORK.

The family lacked the tight-knit community they
had built in Harlem to help them during rough
times. Not even the Black Panthers supported the
Shakurs during their stint in Baltimore.

The only positive development that came out
of their impoverished situation was that 13-year-
old Tupac and nine-year-old Sekyiwa got to spend
more time with their mom. Without her activist

work and job, Afeni became a stay-at-home mom for the first time. She devoted more time than ever to her children, participating in school functions and other activities. Yet, she had a hard time finding employment in Baltimore, and the family had to go on welfare.

In the new city, Tupac remained interested in music. He started rapping in a New York-influenced style about issues that were important to African-American teens, especially those living in the ghetto. Under the name MC New York, he began to "rhyme with a vengeance" about safe sex, violence between African Americans, and community pride.[2]

BALTIMORE SCHOOL FOR THE ARTS

Tupac had the chance to audition for enrollment at Baltimore School for the Arts and was accepted on a scholarship. At age 15, Tupac began at the school as a sophomore. Tupac seized the prestigious opportunity with fervor. He continued writing lyrics and continued writing poetry. He developed a unique poetic style through which he talked about his personal experience as a young, African-American male. His poetry from this time period has become well known. It is even used when teaching poetry to high school and college students.

In addition to being exposed to ballet, modern dance, musical theater, classical music, and drama at school, students at the Baltimore School for the Arts were taken on field trips to see Broadway plays. Around this time, Tupac had the chance to listen to different kinds of popular music, such as Pink Floyd and David Bowie. For the first time in his life, he was hanging out with people who were very rich. A few of his classmates were even royalty from other countries.

Tupac continued to excel in acting at Baltimore School for the Arts. He even combined acting and rapping to perform pieces such as "Babies Having Babies," about the problem of teen pregnancy. Through acting,

Hip-Hop Music

Historians generally agree that hip-hop music was created by African Americans in the Bronx, New York, in the 1970s. As a lyric-based musical style, artists rapped and sang about issues facing them, including poverty, violence, injustice, and the quest for peace. In the 1980s, New York hip-hop music was dominated by songs about a partying and free-spirited lifestyle. Break dancing and graffiti art became part of the hip-hop culture. By the 1990s, a new form of hip-hop music had developed that focused more on the harsh realities of inner-city life, including violence, drugs, poverty, and gangs. The music became known as gangsta rap.

Tupac began rapping in the late 1980s, and his style bridged the party sound with the emerging gangsta-rap style. Like the original hip-hop artists of the 1970s, Tupac wanted to rap about real issues, and it was important to him that his lyrics told a meaningful story.

▲ TUPAC WAS CLOSE FRIENDS WITH JADA PINKETT HIS ENTIRE LIFE.

he met one of his dearest friends, Jada Pinkett, who would later become a famous actress. In his poem "Jada," he wrote, "u R my Heart in Human

Form / a Friend I could never replace."[3] The two remained good friends for the rest of Tupac's life.

During this time, he also developed a close friendship with a white classmate named John Cole. The two had grown up in completely different worlds. Tupac often stayed over at John's house, where he got a taste of wealth and privilege that he had not experienced in his own home. John and his friends could drink and eat whatever they wanted as well as use the stereo and television however they pleased. Despite these differences in upbringing, John and Tupac formed a strong bond. Both had grown up without fathers. They supported each other during difficult times. For John, Tupac wrote the poem "Nothing Can Come Between Us."

Tupac's interest in politics and community activism intensified during high school. He met an organizer named Truxon Sykes, who had started an antigun violence campaign called "Yo-No." Tupac was very active in the campaign. He passed out flyers and performed at churches and schools to spread the campaign's message.

NOTICING CLASS DIFFERENCES
Despite his love for his school, his new friends there, and the many creative outlets it provided, Tupac became increasingly bothered by the

differences in wealth he witnessed every day. At his private school, most of the students were "white kids and rich minorities."[4] They were well read with nice clothes and cars. When Tupac went home to the ghetto at night, he saw poverty and crime. He recalled, "I loved my childhood but I hated growing up poor, and it made me very bitter. We live in hell. We live in the gutter, a war zone."[5]

"i exist in the depths
  of solitude
pondering my true goal
Trying 2 find peace of mind
and still preserve my
  soul"[6]
        —an excerpt from the
    poem "In the Depths of
    Solitude" by Tupac Shakur

In addition to living in the ghetto, the family was under other stresses. Afeni had begun using drugs. The family continued to be tailed by an FBI officer until the FBI finally caught and arrested Mutulu, who was sentenced to 60 years in prison. Meanwhile, Tupac's other father figure, Legs, was released from prison. Shortly after, however, he died of a heart attack as a result of smoking crack cocaine, a powerfully addictive and dangerous street drug.

The striking difference between Tupac's life at school and his life at home became too much to bear. He was especially troubled by the violence between African Americans, which he felt the mainstream media misrepresented:

▲ IN HIS FUTURE ROLE IN THE FILM *JUICE*, TUPAC, *SECOND FROM LEFT*, PLAYED A CHARACTER SIMILAR TO HIMSELF—A BOY WHO GREW UP IN A ROUGH NEIGHBORHOOD.

The same crime element that white people fear, we fear. So we defend ourselves with the same crime element that they scared of. . . . So while they waiting for legislation to pass, and everything, we next door to the killer. . . . Just cuz we're black we get along with the killers or something? We get along with the rapists cuz we black and we from the same hood? What is that? We need protection too.[7]

Absorbed in inner-city street life by night and reading Shakespeare with rich kids by day proved to be an uncomfortable balancing act. Tupac was bothered that the education system ignored real-life issues to focus on traditional subjects that he often found pointless. He later said,

> *I think there should be a drug class, a sex education class. A class on police brutality. There should be a class on Apartheid. There should be a class on why people are hungry, but there are not. There are classes on . . . gym. Physical education. Let's learn volleyball.*[8]

Nevertheless, when the family decided to leave the ghetto of Baltimore, Tupac was disappointed to leave his school. At 17 years old, Tupac had to quit Baltimore School for the Arts. The family was on their way to a new chapter—one that began in California.

—•◆•—

4

THE START
OF A CAREER

upac's family settled in Marin City, California, in 1988. Though they had moved west to escape the ghettos of Baltimore, Tupac again found himself hanging around rough street hustlers in a poor neighborhood. He attended Tamalpais High School and even became involved with the New Afrikan Panthers, a youth organization that held some of the same ideas as the original Black Panthers.

In the ghetto where the Shakurs lived, many residents used the drug crack cocaine. Much to

▶ TUPAC WANTED TO USE RAP TO DISCUSS THE CHALLENGES AND REALITIES OF AFRICAN-AMERICAN LIFE.

Tupac's and Sekyiwa's heartache, Afeni began smoking the drug, and her use soon developed into an addiction.

Around this time, Tupac dropped out of high school. He did not have enough credits to graduate with his class, and he wanted to start earning a living. He moved in with a group of boys living in an abandoned apartment and began working in a pizza parlor. Without his family, he hung around the streets more often. He was not good at dealing drugs himself, and he believed that the drug industry was used as a way to keep African Americans down. But hustlers often took care of him anyway. They gave him money when he needed it and encouraged him to pursue his dreams.

A WAY TO SPEAK THE TRUTH

During this time, Tupac started making a plan to deal with his frustration with poor African-American neighborhoods. He believed his calling was to tell the truth about the pain, suffering, and violence that consumed communities. After learning the truth, people would be moved to make positive changes. He said,

> So I thought, that's what I'm going to do as an artist, as a rapper. I'm gonna show the

most graphic details of what I see in my community and hopefully they'll stop it quick.[1]

To live out his artistic mission, Tupac would need to become famous. In the spring of 1989, he met Leila Steinberg, who was a teacher and a poet. Steinberg was impressed by Tupac right away. Eventually, she became his manager, and Tupac moved in with her and her family.

Leila Steinberg

With Arabic and Jewish roots, Steinberg had been raised in the African-American ghetto called Watts. She worked as a dancer, a teacher, and a poet and focused on building self-expression among impoverished urban youth. After marrying an African American DJ named Bruce, she began promoting him and planning rap concerts in the Bay Area of San Francisco. This was how she came to know groups such as Digital Underground.

HIS BIG BREAK

With Steinberg's help, Tupac landed a gig performing in front of a huge crowd at the Marin City Festival. There he met Gregory "Shock G" Jacobs, the leader of the rap group Digital Underground. Jacobs liked Tupac because he was down-to-earth. Pretty soon, Tupac was invited to join the group as a roadie and hype-man.

Tupac began adding some of his own verses to Digital Underground's songs. The rappers liked his lyrics, and soon Tupac became a rapper in the

LIVES CUT SHORT

group. By 1990, he was traveling with Digital Underground on a world tour. He recalled this period as "some of the best times of my life."[2] The money Tupac earned on tour allowed him to buy his first car, a Toyota Celica, and to rent an apartment.

Digital Underground released its album *This Is an EP Release* in 1991. On it, Tupac delivered a verse in the popular song "Same Song." People now knew who Tupac was. He had the recognition needed to start his solo project. He intended for his music to be edgier, darker, and more political than Digital Underground's. Fortunately for Tupac, popular rap music was transitioning to a tougher sound. One music label, Interscope Records, was looking for artists who fell in line with this new sound. Tupac fit, and he was signed on as a rapper.

Digital Underground

Digital Underground was an Oakland, California-based hip-hop group that produced lighthearted party hits such as "Doowutchyalike" and "The Humpty Dance." Their sound was influenced by legends including Parliament Funkadelic. The group was headed by Shock G and produced their 1990s records with Tommy Boy Records.

FIRST RUN-INS WITH THE LAW

Although Tupac's career was growing, his personal life hit a difficult patch. He began having run-ins with the law that would continue throughout his life.

▲ TUPAC HAD THE OPPORTUNITY TO BECOME A RAPPER
WITH THE GROUP DIGITAL UNDERGROUND.

On October 17, 1991, he was stopped by two
police officers for jaywalking. The officers began
to hassle him about his name and demanded
identification. Though he complied by providing
three forms, they did not believe it was his real
name. The situation escalated when Tupac angrily
demanded his citation so he could be on his way.
The officers threw him to the ground and began
slamming his face on the pavement and choking
and kicking him. After they beat him, the officers

arrested and jailed Tupac for seven hours for resisting arrest.

Though Tupac sued the City of Oakland for $10 million, he eventually settled for $42,000. Some considered it a small settlement, considering the two officers had a documented history of using unnecessary and excessive force and making false arrests of African-American citizens. Despite this minor legal success, Tupac felt that the scars left on his face were unfortunate proof of what an African-American man had to experience.

The day Tupac was harassed for identification was the same day his music video for

Rodney King and Police Brutality

At the time Tupac experienced his beating by police, another police brutality case was in the public spotlight. On March 3, 1991, Rodney King and some friends were driving on a Los Angeles interstate. King and his friends had been drinking, and when the California Highway Patrol tried to pull them over for speeding, King tried to flee. Once police pulled him over, King resisted arrest. Officers beat him, severely fracturing a facial bone and breaking his leg.

A civilian watching from a nearby home caught the incident on video. The image of an African-American man being hit repeatedly by batons and kicked by white police officers disturbed and enraged people. But when the case went to trial the following year, the jury acquitted the officers. People were outraged that the officers would not go to jail. Riots, which became known as the Los Angeles Riots of 1992, broke out on April 29. More than 50 people were killed, and an estimated $1 billion worth of property was damaged.

▲ IN CALIFORNIA, TUPAC, *RIGHT*, STARTED GETTING IN
TROUBLE WITH THE LAW.

his song "Trapped" debuted on MTV. Ironically,
Tupac was depicted in the video as being a
victim of police brutality. The combination of
controversy and fame would follow Tupac for the
rest of his days.

———•◆•———

5

FAME AND CONTROVERSY

Just one month after the Oakland police incident, Tupac's first solo album, *2Pacalypse Now*, was released on Interscope Records in November 1991. It was immediately popular and eventually sold millions of copies. Tupac's solo music was considered gangsta rap, an increasingly popular style of music that focused on the realities of inner-city street life, such as violence, poverty, and drugs.

Earlier that year, Tupac had auditioned for a part in the film, *Juice*, about a group of streetwise

▶ AFTER THE RELEASE OF HIS FIRST SOLO ALBUM, TUPAC'S RAP CAREER SKYROCKETED.

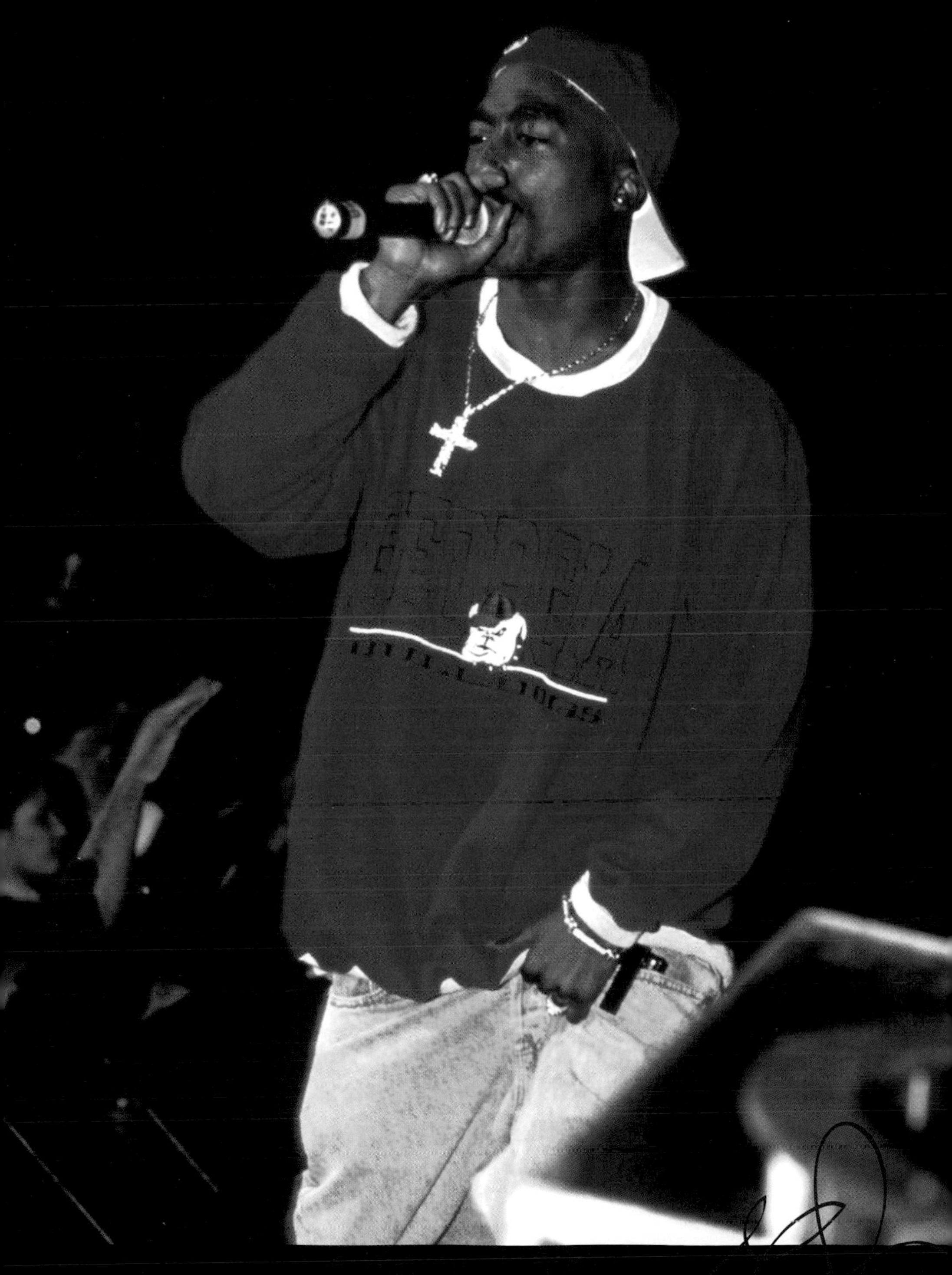

friends from Harlem who try to gain power. Though he had not prepared for the audition, Tupac was cast on the spot as Bishop, an unstable young man who ends up losing his mind and becoming a danger to himself and his friends.

ACTING

The intensity Tupac brought to his role disturbed and impressed audiences. An old high school friend recalled that the look in Tupac's eyes while in character reminded him of something he had seen in Tupac as a teenager: "Blank and distant, disconnected in every way from the situation around him, as if it simply did not exist."[1]

Tupac explained that his acting technique was not about becoming another person but finding the character inside himself:

Gangsta Rap

Gangsta rap began with the release of N.W.A.'s album *Straight Outta Compton* in 1988 and quickly grew in popularity. The music depicted the harsh reality of the streets, including violence and poverty. Lyrics focused on gang life and the prevalence of drugs in inner cities. Another leading artist in gangsta rap, Ice-T, said, "This music isn't supposed to be positive. It's supposed to be negative, because the streets are negative."[2]

Lyrics of gangsta rap are often criticized for describing extreme violence and for being derogatory, or insulting, toward women, who are often treated merely as sex objects. Yet, many listeners often find a connection to the music's subject, and the genre continues to have many supporters.

▲ AN IMAGE FROM *JUICE*, THE FIRST MOVIE IN WHICH
TUPAC, *LEFT*, HAD A MAJOR ROLE

*I don't think acting is as technical as they try
and make it. . . . All you really have to do
is feel for your character and relate to your
character. Because when you act you satisfy
something inside of yourself. The character is
me, I'm Bishop.*[3]

Indeed, each of his roles showed sides of himself
that would emerge in other situations throughout
his life.

When *Juice* was released in January of 1992,
film critics immediately recognized Tupac's

influence. One critic even called him "the film's most magnetic figure."[4] At just 20 years old, Tupac was a star.

More acting roles quickly came his way. He reunited with Jada Pinkett for a few episodes of the popular sitcom *A Different World,* a spin-off of *The Cosby Show.* He was cast as Lucky in the John Singleton film *Poetic Justice,* about a young woman struggling to make it in South Central Los Angeles. The film used poems by Maya Angelou, a writer whom Tupac read and admired. In the movie, he costarred with Janet Jackson. The two became friends, and their on-screen chemistry made the film successful.

Lucky was a very different character from Bishop. He was a responsible, working father doing his best to care for his young daughter. In *Poetic Justice,* Tupac was able to show the side of himself that was sensitive to the lives of young, poor African-American women. He had always felt that he was an advocate for women, mainly due to his upbringing by a strong and politically active single mother. "I think my mother taught me to understand women a lot more than my peers can," he explained. "If you're raised by a woman, you're going to have feminine characteristics."[5]

His respect for women and their experiences led him to write "Keep Ya Head Up," released in 1993. The song was intended to show respect for young women as well as empower them. Tupac also had many female friends throughout his life. He said,

> *I have respect for women. Ultra respect for women. I like being around females, I'm comfortable. I can get with them on every level. I don't get like a predator thing going on when I'm around a demure female, and I'm not uncomfortable around strong women.*[6]

Positive Message for Women

In "Keep Ya Head Up," Tupac gave women a positive message. He told women to leave the men they are with if they are not treated with the respect they deserve. But he also had a message for men, saying they should value the women in their lives. His lyrics addressed the many hardships women faced and acknowledged that the situation should be different.

BLAME AND CRITICISM

Tupac was a rising star, but not everyone welcomed his success. Gangsta rap was a focus in the political debate between conservatives and liberals, and Tupac was about to become its representative. In April 1992, a young car thief named Ronald Ray Howard shot and killed a Texas state trooper. Howard's defense attorney claimed that Tupac's song "Soulja's Story" was

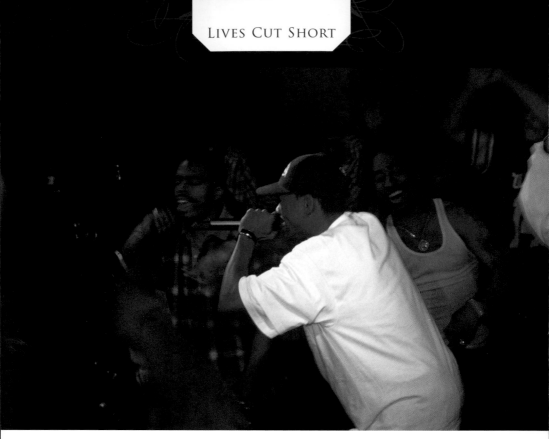

▲ TUPAC, *RIGHT*, PERFORMING WITH FELLOW RAPPERS IN 1995

playing in Howard's car at the time of the murder. He said that the song, in which Tupac raps about killing a cop, caused Howard to commit the crime. The defense did not hold up, however, and Howard was convicted of murder and sentenced to death. Yet Tupac's first experience with public relations trouble on account of his music would not be his last.

Soon after the Texas murder, Tupac faced another serious situation. Following one of his performances in Marin City in August 1992,

Tupac and his friends got into a fight with their rivals. Shots were fired, and a stray bullet hit a six-year-old child in the head. The little boy died soon after. The boy's parents sued Tupac for wrongful death, as the bullet allegedly came from Tupac's gun. It was later proven that Tupac did not fire the gun. Still, Interscope Records intervened on Tupac's behalf and settled with the boy's family.

Tupac's reputation as a dangerous influence was growing in the eyes of mainstream society. In a well-publicized speech, Vice President Dan Quayle said of *2Pacalypse Now*, "There's no reason for a record like this to be released. It has no place in our society."[7] Other well-known conservative politicians, such as radio commentator Rush Limbaugh and U.S. Senator Bob Dole, also spoke out against gangsta rap and Tupac. These politicians believed that the music glorified guns and killing. Tupac lightly dismissed Bob Dole and his criticism: "I don't got no disrespect towards

Censorship of Rap

When Ronald Ray Howard's lawyers blamed Howard's crime of shooting a police officer on the lyrics of gangsta rappers such as Tupac, censorship of gangsta rap became a hot topic in the news. Gangsta rappers argued that, like other artists, they were merely rapping about the reality of their lives. They argued they had the right to include all the harsh details. Supporters of censorship argued that rap was actually creating a culture of violence by making it seem cool to young listeners.

Bob Dole. . . . He's just talking, some card that somebody gave him, he's just reading off that card. . . . he's cute, you know. . . . He's like my grandfather."[8]

But it was not only white male conservatives who were concerned about gangsta rap's influence on young people. Influential members of the African-American community, such as civil rights leaders Jesse Jackson and C. Delores Tucker, were also offended by the style and lyrics of gangsta rap. As writer Khepra Burns said of Tupac's lyrics, "What I hear generally are words that rip through our communities, our families, and our lives like automatic weapon fire."[9] Still others, such as singer Dionne Warwick, spoke out against the portrayal of women in rap videos. In her opinion, women were treated as sexual objects or playthings, which encouraged sexual violence. Although Tupac had written songs to empower women, like "Keep Ya Head Up," his other songs and videos regularly featured language and situations that many people felt degraded women.

"When did I ever say I was a gangsta rapper? Is Frank Sinatra a gangsta singer? Is Steven Seagal a gangsta actor? . . . That's such a limited term. . . . I'm an artist. And I rap about the oppressed taking back their place. I rap about fighting back. To me, my lyrics and my verses are about struggling and overcoming."[10]
—Tupac Shakur

▲ C. DELORES TUCKER, STANDING BESIDE THE COVER ART OF ONE OF TUPAC'S ALBUMS, WAS A STRONG CRITIC OF TUPAC'S MUSIC.

While Tupac took much of the political commentary in stride, he could not take his new status as a role model for young African-American men lightly. He was beginning to feel a responsibility as the voice and leader of a generation that was suffering from violence and poverty. Now, more than ever, he wanted to make his mark on the streets.

6

THUG LIFE

*E*ven though Tupac was quickly gaining fame, he felt it was important to stay true to his beliefs. He wanted to continue connecting with the African-American community and also spread his ideas to a wider audience. Tupac was beginning to build a concept called "thug life" that would do just that.

Tupac defined *thug* differently from a dictionary, which usually defines the word as a criminal. Tupac used the word to represent an underdog or outsider in society, but someone who still takes pride in himself or herself.

▶ AS TUPAC'S POPULARITY GREW, HE ATTENDED MORE PARTIES AND EVENTS.

He described it this way: "I call thugs the nobodies, because we really don't have nobody to help us but us. And then outlaw is being black and minority. Period."[1]

Thug life was the belief that African-American communities were suffering from racist and classist government and educational systems. The systems tore such communities apart by causing internal violence and keeping poverty as a standard way of life.

Tupac believed that an underground economy could be developed to change this. The economy would be based on illegal activity, such as dealing drugs, to make money and uplift African-American communities. Similar to the Black Panthers of his childhood, Tupac believed that violence was acceptable under certain circumstances.

Even though violence and illegal activity were a part of thug life, some positive ideas were behind it as well. Tupac's approach included a message to kids that education and intelligence were important. Tupac prepared a code of ethics, or rules, that described appropriate and inappropriate behavior for carrying out thug life. He hoped the code would help keep its participants and their communities safe.

Tupac saw the prevalence of thug life across the country. He once said, "I don't understand why America doesn't understand thug life. America *is* thug life."[2] To him, thug life was reality; it was inner-city life that millions experienced every day. Tupac became so involved in the thug life concept that he had the words tattooed across his stomach.

> ### Code of Thug Life
>
> Tupac felt strongly that a code of ethics should hold thug life followers to a certain standard. Participants were supposed to protect women, children, and the elderly. This included not selling drugs to children, not selling in schools, and not selling to pregnant women. Another rule was that followers of thug life should not take part in unnecessary violence, such as drive-by shootings.

LEADING YOUNG AFRICAN AMERICANS

Tupac was a powerful and charismatic speaker and performer. He was selling out concerts, and his message was spreading quickly. At 22 years old, he was contacted by gang and criminal leaders around the country to lead the young generation of African-American males. Tupac thought it was a challenging yet valuable task:

> *I was from a single mother. With no father, no male figure. Now I got every man in America who wants to take an order from me . . . who wants to know what I want to do, or what's my plan for young, black males. And that makes*

▲ ONE OF TUPAC'S SEVERAL TATTOOS WERE THE WORDS
"THUG LIFE" ACROSS HIS STOMACH.

me scared. But that makes me want to rise to
the occasion. Makes me wanna give my whole
life to 'em.[3]

He did rise to the occasion. Tupac shared
his thoughts and ideas at his concerts and in
interviews and by speaking at events such as the
Indiana Black Expo of 1993.

MORE RUN-INS WITH THE LAW

Meanwhile, Tupac was getting in trouble with the law. As he once famously said, "I had no record all my life . . . no police record until I made a record."[4] Following his first arrest for jaywalking in 1991, Tupac was arrested on three consecutive assault charges in 1993. In March, he got in a fight with a limo driver on the way to a taping for the television show *In Living Color*. Tupac felt the driver was racist and disrespectful to him and his friend. The charges were later dropped. That same month he got into a fistfight with two film directors who had fired him from a movie they had promised to him. The case resulted in 15 days in jail for Tupac. His third offense occurred when he got into a fight with another rapper and attacked him with a baseball bat during a concert in April. Tupac was arrested again and given ten days in jail. But his run-ins with the law would get even more serious.

In Atlanta, Georgia, in October 1993, Tupac was arrested for the serious aggravated assault of two off-duty police officers. He and his friends had gotten into a fight with the men, unaware that they were police officers. Shots were fired. The officers claimed Tupac had pulled a gun and shot at them, while Tupac claimed one of the men shot at him first. The charges were dropped once it was determined that the men failed to identify themselves as police officers, were drunk, and possessed a stolen gun.

One month later, Tupac encountered what would result in his greatest legal difficulty and personal turmoil yet. In November, a female fan accused Tupac and three other men of sexually assaulting her in a hotel room. Police officers arrived at the hotel to arrest Tupac and the others, who were charged with rape and weapons possession. Bail was set at $50,000. Tupac pleaded innocent. He said he was in another room asleep when the assault happened. However, he did feel responsible for leaving the woman alone with the men who harmed her. He would endure a very public trial for the crime.

Speech at the Expo

The Indiana Black Expo is a large annual event to celebrate African-American families and culture and to talk about issues that are important to African-American communities, such as improving health care and economic conditions. Several celebrities attended the 1993 event at which Tupac spoke, including famous soul singer Patti LaBelle and George Clinton of Parliament Funkadelic.

At the Expo, Tupac delivered an impassioned speech about thug life. In it, Tupac called the entire African-American community—rich and poor—thugs. He stressed that while others thought of the word *thug* as negative, their community could give it a positive connotation. He said that thug life was a "new kind of black power."[5]

CONTINUING TO ACT AND RAP

Tupac continued to receive acting roles, but his increasingly negative reputation as a violent person sometimes made life difficult for him on movie sets. Producers were nervous about working with him, and they sometimes rejected him or dropped him from projects. Regardless, he had a chance to star as a drug dealer named Birdie in the successful independent film *Above the Rim*, which was released in 1994. He also played Tank in the 1996 crime thriller *Bullet* opposite Mickey Rourke. He and Rourke got along well, and the two became friends.

In 1994, Tupac put out an album named after his life philosophy, *Thug Life, Volume 1*, which included song collaborations with several other big-name rappers. It went gold. Meanwhile, Tupac's song "Pour Out a Little Liquor" had been featured on the soundtrack for the movie *Above the Rim*. The soundtrack album, released by Death Row Records, sold so many copies that it went double platinum. This got Tupac noticed

Albums Sold and Awards

The Recording Industry Association of America tracks the number of music albums sold. The organization places a respected honor on albums that have sold a certain number. Gold means 500,000 albums sold; platinum means 1 million albums sold; multiple-platinum means the album has sold more than 2 million copies; and diamond means an album has sold 10 million copies.

by Death Row Records' powerful cofounder, Suge Knight. Tupac later signed a deal with Death Row Records.

No matter how well he did musically and in film, however, the public eye seemed to stay focused on his affiliation with thug life and on his legal trouble. This prompted talk show host Arsenio Hall's comment that Tupac was "not only one of today's most talented new stars, but one of today's most talked-about new stars."[6] Tupac's music—again, the controversial song "Soulja's Story"—was being used in the defense of two teenagers who were being tried for shooting and killing a police officer in September 1994. Once again, the argument was that they had been influenced by the song to commit the crime.

Tupac was frustrated that he was being seen as a bad influence. Comparing himself to white filmmaker Quentin Tarantino, whose movies are notoriously violent and bloody, Tupac said,

> *When he puts out his pictures, they're all gangster pictures and they're all good and they're all critically acclaimed . . . and they're very creative. But when we do that same thing . . . just as compelling . . . we get treated like the bad messengers and he gets treated like King Solomon.*[7]

▲ TUPAC, *CENTER*, PLAYED A DRUG DEALER IN *ABOVE THE RIM*.

Differences in public perception of white and African-American art would not be the only problem Tupac would have to confront in the next years. Unfortunately for him, the worst was yet to come.

———— •◆• ————

7

CRIME AND VIOLENCE

In the midst of all his legal turmoil, one of Tupac's wishes came true. His mom, Afeni, overcame her drug addiction. She became part of his life again. Afeni was by Tupac's side while he busily worked on a new album called *Me Against the World*. Her presence was a comfort to him, and he quickly forgave her for her absence in the previous years. He wrote the song "Dear Mama" to show his appreciation and love for her. It included the lines, "And even as a crack fiend, mama / You always was a black queen, mama."[1]

▶ TUPAC WAS ARRESTED IN NOVEMBER 1993 ON SEXUAL ASSAULT CHARGES.

▲ AFENI, *LEFT*, SPENT A LOT OF TIME WITH TUPAC AFTER
RECOVERING FROM HER DRUG ADDICTION.

It ended up becoming a Number 1 song from the
album.

Though his mom was finally clean, Tupac
had developed a marijuana habit. Later, he would
look back on his use of marijuana and alcohol
and connect it to some of the poor decisions he
made during the early 1990s.

Tupac's trial for sexual assault charges began
in late 1994. His reputation as a gangsta rapper

with a criminal record played a part in the trial. Cameras followed him before and after hearings, and the media covered the trial on prime-time television. The stress upset Tupac, and he continued his heavy marijuana use. He also experienced depression and paranoia and said, "I went through this and I didn't blow my brains out like Kurt Cobain, and I should have because this is some crazy, crazy, crazy madness."[2] As had happened to rock star Cobain, unwanted media attention and drug use were making Tupac's unstable mental state worse. He felt trapped by society's image of him.

SHOT AND ROBBED

On November 29, 1994—one year after the incident in the hotel and the night before his verdict was read—Tupac was headed to Quad Recording Studio in New York's Times Square with a few friends to record a song. Rapper Notorious B.I.G., commonly called Biggie, would be joining them there. Biggie and Tupac had become good friends a few years before. Tupac respected Biggie's talent, and the two had begun recording songs together.

When Tupac and his friends arrived just after midnight on November 30, several guys wearing army fatigues were waiting in the lobby. At first

Tupac did not take much notice because some of Biggie's friends dressed that way. But as Tupac tried to enter the elevator, the strangers pulled out guns, demanding that he and his buddies get on the floor and take off their jewelry. Though Tupac's friends jumped to the floor, Tupac resisted, and the men shot him in the leg and groin. After the first shot, Tupac lay there, trying to play dead. They shot him four more times in the head, groin, hand, and thigh, where the bullet hit an artery. He soon went unconscious.

Once Tupac regained consciousness, he was in the studio and robbed of his money and jewelry, which totaled approximately $40,000. Biggie and another rapper named Sean Combs, then known as Puff Daddy, were there. Later when Tupac recalled that moment, he felt that the way they looked at him and acted during the event seemed suspicious. It seemed as if they had set him up. Within weeks of the shooting, Tupac became convinced that Biggie and Puff Daddy had been involved. He thought they had arranged the shooting because he had refused to sign on with their label, Bad Boy Records.

In the very least, Tupac felt that they had known something was coming and should have warned him. Although Biggie and Puff Daddy

▲ BEFORE TUPAC WAS SHOT, HE AND BIGGIE, *LEFT*, HAD BEEN FRIENDS.

claimed that they were just as shocked as he was by the shooting, Tupac did not believe them. In addition, he was disturbed that fellow African Americans had attacked him. He said, "Until it happened, I really did believe that no black person would ever shoot me. I believed that I didn't have to fear my own community."[3] No one was ever arrested for the shooting. Not only had Tupac's body been wounded in the incident—his sense of trust was injured as well.

The first police officer Tupac saw when he regained consciousness was the one who had arrested him when he was accused of rape. Tupac noted that the officer seemed to sneer at his groin injury. Tupac was rushed to Bellevue Hospital, where doctors performed emergency surgery. His family and many other visitors, including former Black Panthers and other members of the African-American liberation movement, came to see Tupac at the hospital. Hundreds of fans congregated outside. The most surprising visitor, however, was a man named Billy Garland, who Tupac learned was his biological father. Tupac had met him only once as a young boy and did not know then that Garland was his father. In fact, growing up Tupac

East Coast versus West Coast

The shooting of Tupac at Quad Recording Studio sparked the feud between West Coast and East Coast rappers. Death Row Records represented rappers on the West Coast, and Bad Boy Records represented rappers on the East Coast.

Tupac believed Biggie and Puff Daddy were behind his shooting. In his song "Hit 'Em Up," Tupac voiced his suspicions about Biggie's and Puff Daddy's involvement, claimed he had slept with Biggie's wife, and insulted the rappers on Bad Boy Records. Biggie countered with a song called "Who Shot Ya," which seemed to mock Tupac's accusations and celebrated East Coast rap. Biggie denied the song was about Tupac, pointing out that it had been recorded before the shooting, but Tupac said that even if it was not about him, it was wrong of Biggie to release the song when he did.

The feud continued throughout Tupac's and Biggie's lives, spreading to rappers outside the representative record labels.

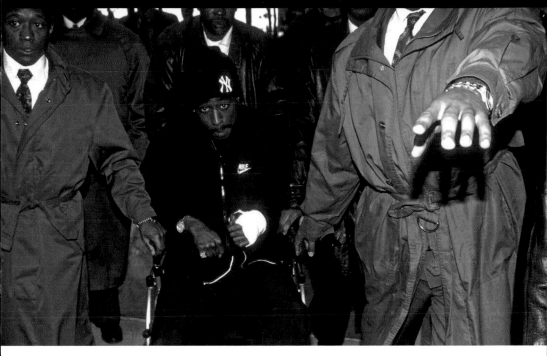

▲ TUPAC ARRIVED AT THE COURTHOUSE IN A WHEELCHAIR
THE DAY AFTER HE WAS SHOT.

thought his real father must be dead. But Garland
was at the hospital, and the two looked alike.

At the time, Tupac was suffering from extreme
paranoia. According to Afeni, when Tupac saw
his father he thought he had seen his own ghost.
Though Tupac was in critical condition, he
disconnected himself from the IVs and left the
hospital. The constant phone calls, visitors, and
the shock of the shooting made him nervous and
more paranoid—he worried that the police would
come and kill him. He recalled feeling like a
"prisoner . . . [of his] own fame."[4]

SENTENCING TO PRISON

Though Tupac had only been out of surgery for 12 hours and had been excused from his court hearing, he decided to attend anyway. He was found guilty on three counts of sexual abuse and innocent on six other charges, including weapons possession. While he waited for his sentencing, he recovered at the New York City apartment of friend and actress Jasmine Guy, along with his mother, Aunt Gloria, and his cousins.

Several people provided testimonies to help lessen Tupac's sentence. People recalled his many donations of his time and his money. He had donated to the Make-A-Wish Foundation, as well as to other organizations that helped those in need. In the end, he was sentenced to one-and-a-half to four-and-a-half years in prison. Prison would

Notorious B.I.G.

When Tupac and Biggie first met, they felt a connection. Both were familiar with street life, were raised by single mothers, and brought the gritty reality of poverty and violence into their music.

In 1994, Biggie, whose real name was Christopher Wallace, released his first album, *Ready to Die*, on Bad Boy Records. The album was a raw look at the reality of street life. Biggie quickly became Bad Boy Records' number-one artist. When Tupac's and Biggie's relationship turned sour, Biggie became Tupac's East Coast enemy in the East Coast–West Coast rapper feud.

Similar to Tupac, Biggie was killed in a drive-by shooting on March 9, 1997, when he was 25 years old. His second album, *Life After Death*, was released just 15 days after his death. He is regarded as a hip-hop legend whose life tragically ended at the height of his success.

▲ IN LATE 1994, TUPAC WAS FOUND GUILTY OF SEXUAL
ASSAULT AND SENTENCED TO PRISON.

offer a time of reflection, sobriety, writing, and
a separation from the lifestyle Tupac had been
living during the past few years. He would try to
get back to what truly mattered.

—•◆•—

8

PRISON AND A
NEW BEGINNING

n February 1995, Tupac began serving his prison sentence. He would do the majority of his time at a maximum-security prison in upstate New York called Clinton Correctional Facility, where the most dangerous killers, gangsters, and criminals went. Tupac's fame did not protect him from mistreatment by the guards, however. Right away they smacked him around and called him racist names. He quickly learned that society's norms against using racial slurs did not apply in prison. The facility was also

▸ TUPAC ORIGINALLY THOUGHT GOING TO PRISON WAS A
NATURAL STEP FOR AFRICAN-AMERICAN MEN.

▲ WHILE IN PRISON, TUPAC OFTEN SAW VIOLENCE AND HEARD RACIAL SLURS.

unsafe—Tupac witnessed two murders during his time there.

Shortly into his sentence, however, he learned how to survive and came to view prison like a business. Through secretive money exchanges and trades, he could get along with his fellow inmates. He was surprised to find that he even became

friendly with a skinhead—
Tupac even signed his
autograph for the skinhead's
nieces and nephews. Though
the two men might have
hated each other in the
outside world, they bonded
in prison.

Going to prison so soon
after being almost killed had
turned Tupac away from the
rap scene. He thought about
quitting rapping forever. In
any case, he was not able
to write music while he
was imprisoned. He said, "My inspiration was
gone because I was a caged animal."[1] But he did
make time for other creative pursuits. He wrote
a screenplay called *Live 2 Tell*. He practiced
meditation and martial arts techniques and
worked out in his cell. He wrote long letters to
friends, family, and love interests. He read the
poetry of Maya Angelou, Niccolò Machiavelli's
The Prince, and *The Art of War,* an ancient
Chinese book on military strategy by Sun Tzu. A
few celebrity friends, such as civil rights activist
Al Sharpton and actor Tony Danza, visited him.

Al Sharpton

Al Sharpton was a close friend of Tupac. The Baptist minister and African-American leader has been a prominent figure speaking on behalf of civil rights in the tradition of Martin Luther King Jr. He has been recognized by the National Association for the Advancement of Colored People and by Jesse Jackson for his contributions to the African-American liberation movement. He has also been arrested for activity during protests.

In addition to doing hundreds of push-ups, jumping jacks, and sit-ups daily, Tupac was forced to detox from all the alcohol and marijuana he had been consuming in the years before his imprisonment. Getting off the drugs made his mind clearer, and his sense of purpose became stronger. He was also eating as healthfully as possible, avoiding caffeine and red meat.

A NEW WAY OF THINKING

Perhaps most importantly, Tupac started to replace his allegiance to thug life with a new plan for youth across the country. He repeated a phrase from Black Panther Eldridge Cleaver, "You're either part of the solution or part of the problem," and he wanted to be part of the solution.[2] His plan was to open youth centers in every ghetto in the United States. At the youth centers, children could come to play music, make art, read, and learn. His program would be called US FIRST, and he would raise money through his celebrity network to get it done.

Tupac had always felt that going to prison was "part of being a man."[3] When he actually found himself there, however, he realized the experience was not a necessary step of life. Still, he used his time well and admitted that prison taught him important lessons about anger management and

▲ AFENI SHAKUR APPEARED IN THE MUSIC VIDEO FOR
TUPAC'S SONG "DEAR MAMA."

humility. As he made plans for his family's future,
he also began to accept responsibility as the man
of the family.

Before prison, Tupac had begun dating a
woman named Keisha Morris. While Tupac
was in prison, Keisha and Tupac's relationship
grew stronger through letters and visits. On

April 29, 1995, the two were married at Clinton Correctional Facility. Although the marriage was short-lived—it was annulled soon after Tupac's release in October 1995—Tupac and Keisha remained friends. She became another supportive person in Tupac's life.

While Tupac was in prison, his album *Me Against the World* was released. It quickly became Number 1 on the R & B and pop charts. The video for "Dear Mama" featured Afeni. The record went double platinum that year, and Tupac declared that it was his favorite of all the ones he made.

His success prompted new negotiations with Suge Knight of Death Row Records. Though Knight had been trying to recruit

Death Row Records

Suge Knight and rapper Dr. Dre founded the record label Death Row Records in the early 1990s. Knight had a criminal history that followed him into his business pursuits, including assault charges and a lawsuit brought on by cofounder Lydia Harris. In books and films written about the label, Knight is portrayed as a gang member who used threats and violence to intimidate the musicians on his label. The FBI investigated the label for money laundering and gang activity, but no indictments were made.

Knight was in jail in 1996 for violating his parole when the label released Tupac's posthumous record, *The Don Killuminati: The 7 Day Theory*. Knight continued to sign new artists and put out albums from his jail cell. Death Row Records made a substantial amount of money from Tupac's records that were released after his death.

▲ TUPAC, *RIGHT*, SPOKE AT A VOTER REGISTRATION RALLY FOR AFRICAN AMERICANS AFTER HE WAS RELEASED FROM PRISON.

Tupac for years, he finally had something to offer that Tupac could not refuse. Knight would pay the $1.4 million bond that would release Tupac from prison. In exchange, Tupac would join Death Row Records under a contract to make three albums. Tupac was released from prison on October 10, 1995, and was faced again with his old lifestyle.

9

A PROPHECY FULFILLED

When Tupac was released from prison, he celebrated with friends and family. He rejoiced at the simple pleasure of being able to drive down Sunset Boulevard in Los Angeles.

Almost immediately, Tupac returned to the studio. He spent as much time as possible there and was more serious when he worked. Tupac and his new producer, Dr. Dre of the legendary N.W.A., produced the song "California Love." The song was the dance jam of the moment, getting constant radio play. Tupac was in the

▶ ONCE FREED FROM PRISON, TUPAC BEGAN RECORDING MUSIC AGAIN.

TUPAC SHAKUR

public eye once again—this time not for legal trouble but for his music.

Tupac was also working on building his own business, called Euphanasia, which he intended to have produce movies. He also raised money to start A Place Called Home, a Los Angeles-area program that helped kids, similar to his idea of US FIRST. He convinced celebrity friends to give free performances to raise money.

Tupac was soon cast as Spoon in the movie *Gridlock'd*. In the film, his character is on a mission to get clean from drugs but keeps coming up against roadblocks. Shortly after *Gridlock'd*, Tupac was cast in *Gang Related* with an all-star cast that included Jim Belushi. It would be his last role in a film.

Having his family around him at this time was important, especially since he

Dr. Dre and Tupac

Dr. Dre has been at the forefront of the rap scene since he founded the original 1980s rap group, N.W.A. His own lyrics, personal life, and brushes with the law were filled with controversy and sometimes violence, and he produced the music of edgy artists, such as Snoop Dogg and Tupac, on Death Row Records. When he left the label, Tupac began to criticize Dr. Dre publicly.

Dr. Dre has said that Tupac "liked to stir up stuff and then watch it explode in others' faces. That's a hard way to live and a quicker way to die."[1] Though Dr. Dre and Tupac were at odds at the time of Tupac's death, Dr. Dre maintained his respect for Tupac's work ethic.

had started to distrust the friends he had made
through the music industry. Tupac commented
on his new attitude toward outsiders: "I don't
have friends. I have family. You're either my all-
the-way family or just somebody on the outside."[2]
His mother was now a constant presence in his
life. Many of his family members lived with him
at his new condo on Wilshire Boulevard in Los
Angeles.

Snoop Dogg, another Death Row Records
artist and friend of Tupac, also lived in a condo
in the same building. Snoop Dogg was featured
on Tupac's new album, *All Eyez on Me*. Tupac
released *All Eyez on Me* as a double album, and it
soon went platinum. It would eventually become
one of the top-selling hip-hop records of all time.

After this large success, Tupac started working
on a new album, *The Don Killuminati: The 7 Day
Theory*, which would be released under the stage
name Makaveli. The pseudonym was inspired by
Renaissance Italian political philosopher Niccolò
Machiavelli, one of Tupac's favorite writers.
He also wrote songs and made plans for two
additional records, *Supreme Euthanasia* and *R U
Still Down?* Besides music, he was working on an
autobiography titled *Mama's Boy*.

THE FEUD AND PARANOIA

Even though Tupac was hard at work, his feud with Biggie and Puff Daddy seemed to be growing worse. The dispute brought the East Coast rap scene dominated by Bad Boy Records, Puff Daddy, and Biggie against the West Coast rap scene dominated by Death Row Records, Snoop Dogg, and Tupac. At major events like the Source Hip-Hop Awards in 1995, representatives from each coast ridiculed the other side. Tension was growing, and Tupac was on the front line of a brewing battle.

In the meantime, Tupac was becoming more and more frustrated with Knight and Death Row Records. He felt as if Knight was trying to control him and was not giving him enough information about his record sales. Instead of talking openly with Tupac, Knight bought him gifts, such as a new Rolls Royce and a Hummer. This only agitated Tupac more.

Tupac became paranoid again and felt as if people were out to get him. He was sure his life was in danger and even had a prophecy of his own death. Tupac began to wear a bulletproof vest and became afraid to leave his home.

Tupac's thoughts of dying seemed to motivate him to be even more productive. He was hardly sleeping and spent nearly all of his time writing or working on music and other projects. He frequently talked about death and said,

I know I'm gonna die. They have to kill me. Society, the system, the status quo, the evil empire, they have to kill me because of who I am and what I represent. Because I'm a Shakur. My only choice is how I'm gonna die.[3]

Tupac's image of his own death, and how he would be represented after he died, became very important to him. In the video for his song "I Ain't Mad At Cha," he is shot and killed and then goes to heaven to play music with other famous African-American musicians.

Thoughts of dying and becoming a better person were motivations for Tupac to end the East Coast–West Coast feud. He began to work on *One Nation*, an album featuring musicians from both sides. Since he was from New York and Baltimore originally, the feud had never been regional for Tupac. Rather, a personal issue with a few rappers had gotten out of hand. Yet, in 1996, another fight between Tupac's friends and an East Coast group broke out after Tupac's appearance at the MTV Video Music Awards in New York City. Thankfully, the trip to New York was not a total loss, as Tupac was able to make things right with Nas, an East Coast rapper he had issues with in the past.

Tupac's fear of those around him and what lay ahead was noticeable in the way he interacted with his record company. He once said, "Trust nobody. Trust no-bo-dy."[4] When Knight contacted him to go to a Mike Tyson fight in September 1996, he was reluctant to accept. Even though Tupac's song "Wrote the Glory" would play as Tyson entered the ring, Knight had to convince the rapper to go to the match. Finally, Tupac agreed, and they headed to Las Vegas for the September 7 fight.

A TRAGIC NIGHT IN LAS VEGAS

At first, Tupac and Knight had a great time. Tupac was a huge fan and a friend of Tyson, and he enjoyed supporting the fighter. But the night quickly took a turn for the worst.

After the match, Tupac, Knight, and others from Death Row Records walked through the lobby of the MGM Grand Hotel and Casino,

▲ KNIGHT AND TUPAC AT A BOXING MATCH IN LAS VEGAS

where the boxing match had been held. There, they spotted Orlando Anderson, a member of the Los Angeles-based gang the Crips. Anderson was accused of stealing a piece of jewelry from a Death Row Records employee just a few months earlier. Tupac and the others quickly ran over to Anderson and started beating him, knocking him to the ground. Unbeknownst to the men, the beating was being taped by hidden video cameras in the casino. Soon, security approached the scene, and the Death Row Records entourage took off. Tupac escaped to his hotel room at the Luxor Hotel.

Later that night, Knight invited Tupac to see the rap group Run-DMC at Club 662, the club Knight owned in Las Vegas. Tupac was unsure of leaving his hotel. Knight eventually convinced him to go to the show, however. It was a rare night because Tupac was not wearing his bulletproof vest, and the fight had put him on edge.

Knight picked up Tupac outside the Luxor in his black BMW. The car was one in a group of approximately ten that were heading to the club. The group drove down the Las Vegas strip. Then Knight's car stopped at a red light. A Cadillac with four men in it pulled up alongside the passenger seat, where Tupac was sitting. Suddenly, one man in the Cadillac fired a gun into the BMW. Four bullets hit Tupac—in his hand, chest, and hip—while Knight was hit in the head by a flying piece of glass. The Cadillac sped off as soon as the bullets were shot.

When emergency responders arrived, Tupac was immediately rushed to a Nevada hospital, where Afeni and the rest of his family met him. Fans congregated outside the hospital in a vigil attended by Jesse Jackson. Tupac underwent

▲ POLICE TAPE SURROUNDED THE VEHICLE IN WHICH
TUPAC WAS SHOT.

two operations, and one lung was removed. He
nearly died and was resuscitated several times.
Finally, on September 13, 1996, six days after the
shooting, Afeni decided it was time to let Tupac
go. Aunt Gloria kissed Tupac from head to toe,
just as he had described in a song about his death
called "Life Goes On." Then his life support
machines were shut off. At 25 years old, the
influential musician was dead.

——•◆•——

10

A LIFE OF CONTRASTS AND IMPACT

upac's body was cremated, and the ashes were scattered in several of the places that he had called home. These included areas by his mom's house in Atlanta, by his aunt Gloria's farm in North Carolina, in the ocean near Malibu, California, and on 125th Street in Harlem, where Malcolm X had often spoken. Thousands of fans and supporters attended Tupac's memorial services in Atlanta and in New York City. Still, friends, family, and fans were dismayed that no one was arrested for Tupac's death.

▶ TUPAC DIED AT 25 YEARS OLD.

Las Vegas police began an investigation to find the shooter but found few leads. One of the main suspects in the case was Orlando Anderson, the man whom Tupac, Knight, and others beat on the night of Tupac's shooting. The lead soon fizzled, and Anderson was no longer a suspect. It was also thought by some that Tupac's murder could have been related to the East Coast–West Coast rapper feud, but no substantiating evidence was found to prove it. As of 2009, his murder remained unsolved.

POSTHUMOUS WORKS

Shortly after his death, the products of his last year of work and life

Tupac's Prediction?

Did Tupac know he was going to die? Many say he did. Tupac had always had a sense that he was a target and may die young. He idolized famous artists and musicians who had died tragically and was accustomed to violence that killed many people in his hometown communities. He repeatedly featured death and dying in his lyrics, videos, and writing during the year leading up to his death. In the song "Life Goes On," he actually gave instructions for his funeral.

During the months leading up to Tupac's death, his behavior even more strongly indicated a sense of impending death. He was extremely productive, perhaps as if he was trying to accomplish as much as possible while he could. However, he was also extraordinarily reckless. Some would say his lyrical assaults on other rappers were nothing short of a death wish. Finally, he attempted to make peace with several East Coast rappers within the very last months before he was shot. Some believe that indicated a need for closure—Tupac was getting his affairs in order in preparation for his death.

▲ The night after Tupac died, a graffiti artist painted this mural in New York City as a tribute.

began to emerge. The films *Bullet, Gridlock'd,* and *Gang Related* were released in October 1996, January 1997, and October 1997, respectively. Much praise was given to Tupac's performances in the films, and many said he had shown great potential as an actor.

Tupac's album sales have continued steadily since his death. In total, Tupac's album sales have reached $38 million. Additionally, more albums of Tupac's music have been released since his death. Eight albums, including *The Don Killuminati: The 7 Day Theory* and *R U Still*

Down?, were released posthumously, while only four albums were released while he was living. The Guinness Book of World Records lists Tupac as the best-selling rap artist of all time.

Countless books, articles, documentaries, tributes, and references have been made about Tupac since his death. The most well-known documentary about his life, *Tupac: Resurrection,* was released in 2003. The director pieced together clips from Tupac's many interviews, so as to allow Tupac to narrate his own story. The documentary was nominated for an Academy Award in 2004. His life has been used to explore many larger issues, including African-American youth culture and rap as an artistic medium. He inspired the Tupac Amaru Shakur Foundation, which Afeni founded in 1997. The foundation opened the Tupac Amaru Shakur Center for the Arts in Stone Mountain, Georgia, to support creative arts study for youth. The symbol of the foundation is the cross that was tattooed on Tupac's back.

Three years after Tupac was killed and two years after Biggie was killed, the rappers'

Prophetic Poem

Lines from one of Tupac's poems, "In the Event of My Demise," show his belief that he would die young: "I will die before my time Because I feel the shadow's depth So much I wanted to accomplish Before I reached my death"[1]

▲ AFENI REMEMBERING TUPAC ON THE TENTH
ANNIVERSARY OF HIS DEATH

mothers embraced at the 1999 MTV Video
Music Awards. This gesture showed unity. Their
hope was to finally put an end to the violence
between the East Coast and West Coast gangsta
rappers.

LIFE OF CONTRASTS

Tupac's life was full of struggle and love. It was a life of contradictions. Although he used drugs, he wanted to positively impact the African-American community. Although he took part in violent acts, he wanted freedom from violence for youth. As Moorish Temple minister and prisoner Everett Dyson-Bey has said of Tupac's music:

> If you were going on the path of a social activist, there is something for you in his lyrics. If you were on the path of a straight thug, there is something there for you, too.[2]

Though he died tragically, Tupac left the world with powerful music, writing, and philosophy. Tupac has inspired children, especially those who grew up as he did—in the ghettos with few resources other than their own minds. His writing has been used in many classrooms as a new approach for teaching poetry.

For those who have been impacted by his music and his life, he will not be forgotten.

Rumors That Tupac Is Still Alive

Tupac has many die-hard fans who view him as a god-like figure. Some have even speculated that his death was staged and that he is still alive and well. These people have discussed their conspiracy theories on blogs and in online chat rooms. One theory is based on the fact that Tupac's last album, The Don Killuminati: The 7 Day Theory, references Tupac's alter ego, Makaveli, who faked his own death. However, there is no proof that any of these theories are true.

▲ TUPAC WILL BE REMEMBERED BY FANS ALL OVER THE WORLD.

He once said, "I'm not saying I'm going to change the world. But I guarantee that I will spark the brain that will change the world."[3]

TIMELINE

1971	1984	1986
Tupac Amaru Shakur is born on June 16.	Tupac performs at a presidential campaign event for Jesse Jackson.	Tupac begins attending the Baltimore School for the Arts.

1991	1991	1992
In October, Tupac is harassed, beaten, and arrested by Oakland police officers.	Tupac's first solo album, *2Pacalypse Now*, is released by Interscope Records in November.	*Juice*, the first movie in which Tupac has a major role, is released in January.

TUPAC SHAKUR

1989

Tupac meets poet
Leila Steinberg,
who becomes
his manager for
his rap career.

1990

Tupac tours
worldwide with
Digital Underground
as a roadie and
hype-man.

1991

Digital Underground
releases *This Is
an EP Release*,
which features
Tupac rapping in
"Same Song."

1992

The violence of
Tupac's music is used
as a defense for
Ronald Ray Howard,
who shot and
killed a Texas state
trooper in April.

1993

Tupac speaks about
his philosophy of
thug life at the
Indiana Black Expo.

1993

Tupac is arrested
for shooting at
two off-duty police
officers in Atlanta,
Georgia, in October.

TIMELINE

1993

In November,
Tupac is accused of
sexually assaulting
a woman in a
hotel room.

1994

On November 30,
Tupac is shot five
times at the Quad
Recording Studio
in New York City.

1995

In February, Tupac
goes to prison after
being found guilty
on three charges
of sexual abuse.

1996

In February,
Death Row
Records releases
Tupac's album *All
Eyez on Me*.

1996

Tupac is shot in
Las Vegas on
September 7.

1996

Tupac dies on
September 13.

1995

1995

1995

Tupac's album *Me Against the World* is released in March, while he is in prison.

In April, Tupac marries Keisha Morris while in prison. The marriage is annulled six months later.

In October, Tupac signs with Death Row Records and is released from prison.

1997

1997

2003

In October, the film *Gang Related* is released, representing Tupac's last acting role.

Afeni Shakur founds the Tupac Amaru Shakur Foundation.

The Academy Award–nominated documentary of Tupac's life, *Tupac: Resurrection*, is released.

QUICK FACTS

DATE OF BIRTH
June 16, 1971

PLACE OF BIRTH
New York City

DATE OF DEATH
September 13, 1996

PLACE OF DEATH
Las Vegas, Nevada

PARENTS
Afeni Shakur and Billy Garland

MARRIAGE
Keisha Morris (April 1995–October 1995)

CHILDREN
None

CAREER HIGHLIGHTS

Albums

2Pacalypse Now (1991)
Thug Life, Volume 1 (1994)
Me Against the World (1995)
All Eyez on Me (1996)
The Don Killuminati: The 7 Day Theory (1997)
R U Still Down? (Remember Me) (1997)
Still I Rise (1999)
Until the End of Time (2001)
Better Dayz (2002)
Loyal to the Game (2004)
Pac's Life (2006)

Movies

Juice (1992)
Poetic Justice (1993)
Above the Rim (1994)
Bullet (1996)
Gridlock'd (1997)
Gang Related (1997)
Tupac: Resurrection (2003)

QUOTE

"So I thought, that's what I'm going to do as an artist, as a rapper. I'm gonna show the most graphic details of what I see in my community and hopefully they'll stop it quick."
—*Tupac Shakur*

ADDITIONAL RESOURCES

SELECT BIBLIOGRAPHY

Bastfield, Darrin Keith. *Back in the Day: My Life and Times with Tupac Shakur*. Cambridge, MA: Da Capo Press, 2003.

Dyson, Michael Eric. *Holler If You Hear Me*. New York, NY: Basic Civitas Books, 2001.

Hoye, Jacob, and Karolyn Ali, eds. *Tupac: Resurrection 1971–1996*. New York, NY: Atria Books, 2003.

Joseph, Jamal. *Tupac Shakur Legacy*. New York, NY: Atria Books, 2006.

Lazin, Lauren, dir. *Tupac: Resurrection*. DVD. Woodland Hills, CA: Amaru Entertainment Inc., 2003.

Shakur, Tupac Amaru. *The Rose That Grew from Concrete*. New York, NY: Pocket Books, 1999.

FURTHER READING

Ardis, Angela. *Inside a Thug's Heart: With Original Poems and Letters by Tupac Shakur*. New York, NY: Kensington Publishing, 2002.

Higgins, Dalton. *Hip Hop World: A Groundwork Guide*. Toronto, Canada: Groundwood Books, 2009.

Stanley, Tarshia L., ed. *Encyclopedia of Hip Hop Literature*. Santa Barbara, CA: Greenwood Press, 2008.

WEB LINKS

To learn more about Tupac Shakur, visit ABDO Publishing Company online at **www.abdopublishing.com**. Web sites about Tupac Shakur are featured on our Book Links page. These links are routinely monitored and updated to provide the most current information available.

FOR MORE INFORMATION

For more information on this subject, contact or visit the following organizations.

The Hip-Hop Theater Festival

442-D Lorimer Street, #195, Brooklyn, NY 11206
718-497-4282
www.hhtf.org
Combining Tupac's interests of acting and hip-hop, the Hip-Hop Theater Festival serves as an outlet for artists to perform and address social issues surrounding inner-city life. Visitors to the Web site can learn more about the programs and education offered through the organization.

The Tupac Amaru Shakur Foundation

5616 Memorial Drive, Stone Mountain, GA 30083
404-298-4222
www.tasf.org
The Tupac Amaru Shakur Foundation helps young people develop their creative skills. The foundation holds performing arts camps, where young participants foster their talent in areas such as dancing, singing, and writing.

GLOSSARY

activist
Someone who works on behalf of a cause, especially a political one.

Black Panthers
An African-American liberation organization that worked to gain rights for African Americans and the poor, using violence when necessary.

derogatory
Showing disrespect.

genocide
The deliberate killing of a large group of people, especially a racial or ethnic group.

ghetto
A poor, run-down part of a city where minority groups often live.

hip-hop
A genre of music of African-American origin that features rap.

hustler
A salesperson who obtains money through deceptive means.

hype-man
A person who gets a crowd excited before a musician comes onstage to perform.

posthumous
Happening after a person's death.

prophecy
A prediction.

record label
A company that produces music albums.

roadie
A person who helps set up the stage and equipment for a performance.

tenement
A city dwelling that is often run-down and unsafe.

thug
An outsider or underdog who still has pride in his or her life's circumstances.

thug life
Tupac Shakur's philosophy that the African-American community could benefit from a system of organized illegal activity.

SOURCE NOTES

Chapter 1. Taking the Stage
1. Lauren Lazin, dir. *Tupac: Resurrection.* DVD. Amaru
Entertainment Inc., 2003.

Chapter 2. Growing Up on the Streets
1. Jacob Hoye and Karolyn Ali, eds. *Tupac: Resurrection 1971–
1996.* New York, NY: Atria Books, 2003. 16.
2. Ibid. 6.
3. Ibid. 14.
4. Ibid. 24.
5. Ibid.
6. Ibid. 11.
7. Ibid. 12.

Chapter 3. New City, Same Struggle
1. Jacob Hoye and Karolyn Ali, eds. *Tupac: Resurrection 1971–
1996.* New York, NY: Atria Books, 2003. 34.
2. Jamal Joseph. *Tupac Shakur Legacy.* New York, NY: Atria Books,
2006. 17.
3. Tupac Amaru Shakur. *The Rose That Grew from Concrete.* New
York, NY: Pocket Books, 1999. 89.
4. Jacob Hoye and Karolyn Ali, eds. *Tupac: Resurrection 1971–
1996.* New York, NY: Atria Books, 2003. 54.
5. Ibid. 54.
6. Tupac Amaru Shakur. *The Rose That Grew from Concrete.* New
York, NY: Pocket Books, 1999. 5.
7. Jacob Hoye and Karolyn Ali, eds. *Tupac: Resurrection 1971–
1996.* New York, NY: Atria Books, 2003. 54.
8. Ibid. 63.

Chapter 4. The Start of a Career
1. Jacob Hoye and Karolyn Ali, eds. *Tupac: Resurrection 1971–
1996.* New York, NY: Atria Books, 2003. 70.
2. Lauren Lazin, dir. *Tupac: Resurrection.* DVD. Amaru
Entertainment Inc., 2003.

Chapter 5. Fame and Controversy

1. Darrin Keith Bastfield. *Back in the Day: My ife and Times with Tupac Shakur.* Cambridge, MA: Da Capo Press 2003. 73.
2. John M. Hagedorn. *A World of Gangs: Arme Young Men and Gangsta Culture.* Minneapolis, MN: University f Minnesota Press, 2008. 97.
3. Jacob Hoye and Karolyn Ali, eds. *Tupac: Res rection 1971–1996.* New York, NY: Atria Books, 2003. 85.
4. Janet Maslin. Review of *Juice.* "Too Much to rove, and No Reason to Prove It." *New York Times.* 17 Januar 1992. 25 Aug. 2009 <http://movies.nytimes.com/movie/reviev ?res=9E0CE7DF1 53FF934A25752C0A964958260>.
5. Jacob Hoye and Karolyn Ali, eds. *Tupac: Res rection 1971–1996.* New York, NY: Atria Books, 2003. 93.
6. Ibid. 90.
7. Lauren Lazin, dir. *Tupac: Resurrection.* DVD. maru Entertainment Inc., 2003.
8. Ibid.
9. Michael Eric Dyson. *Holler If You Hear Me.* N w York, NY: Basic Civitas Books, 2001. 123.
10. Jacob Hoye and Karolyn Ali, eds. *Tupac: Res rection 1971–1996.* New York, NY: Atria Books, 2003. 132.

Chapter 6. Thug Life

1. Michael Eric Dyson. *Holler If You Hear Me.* N w York, NY: Basic Civitas Books, 2001. 113.
2. Jacob Hoye and Karolyn Ali, eds. *Tupac: Resur ction 1971–1996.* New York, NY: Atria Books, 2003. 122.
3. Lauren Lazin, dir. *Tupac: Resurrection.* DVD. A naru Entertainment Inc., 2003.
4. Jacob Hoye and Karolyn Ali, eds. *Tupac: Resurr tion 1971–1996.* New York, NY: Atria Books, 2003. 80.
5. Lauren Lazin, dir. *Tupac: Resurrection.* DVD. A naru Entertainment Inc., 2003.
6. Ibid.
7. Michael Eric Dyson. *Holler If You Hear Me.* Ne York, NY: Basic Civitas Books, 2001. 126–127.

SOURCE NOTES
CONTINUED

Chapter 7. Crime and Violence
1. Tupac Shakur. "Dear Mama" lyrics. 4 Aug. 2009 <http://www.lyrics.com/lyrics/2pac/dear-mama.html>.
2. Lauren Lazin, dir. *Tupac: Resurrection*. DVD. Amaru Entertainment Inc., 2003.
3. Ibid.
4. Ibid.

Chapter 8. Prison and a New Beginning
1. Jacob Hoye and Karolyn Ali, eds. *Tupac: Resurrection 1971–1996*. New York, NY: Atria Books, 2003. 156.
2. Jamal Joseph. *Tupac Shakur Legacy*. New York, NY: Atria Books, 2006. 41.
3. Lauren Lazin, dir. *Tupac: Resurrection*. DVD. Amaru Entertainment Inc., 2003.

Chapter 9. A Prophecy Fulfilled
1. Michael Eric Dyson. *Holler If You Hear Me*. New York, NY: Basic Civitas Books, 2001. 169.
2. Jamal Joseph. *Tupac Shakur Legacy*. New York, NY: Atria Books, 2006. 49.
3. Ibid. 46.
4. Jacob Hoye and Karolyn Ali, eds. *Tupac: Resurrection 1971–1996*. New York, NY: Atria Books, 2003. 186.

Chapter 10. A Life of Contrasts and Impact
1. Tupac Amaru Shakur. *The Rose That Grew from Concrete*. New York, NY: Pocket Books, 1999. 150.
2. Michael Eric Dyson. *Holler If You Hear Me*. New York, NY: Basic Civitas Books, 2001. 128.
3. Jamal Joseph. *Tupac Shakur Legacy*. New York, NY: Atria Books, 2006. 61.

INDEX

NDEX
CONTINUED

ABOUT THE AUTHOR

Ashley Rae Harris is a freelance writer who lives and works in Chicago, Illinois. She has a master's degree from the University of Chicago, where she focused her research on youth culture and identity. She has written several books on the topic of adolescent self-esteem, as well as articles for various magazines and online publications, including *Venuszine* and *Time Out Chicago*.

PHOTO CREDITS

Ron Galella/Getty Images, cover, 3; Al Pereira/Getty Images, 7, 9, 41; Photofest, 11, 33, 54, 65, 89; iStockphoto, 13; AP Images, 15; Paramount/Photofest, 19, 30, 39, 43, 96 (top), 96 (bottom); Ingrid Froehlich/IPOL, Inc./Globe Photos, Inc., 21; Bonnie Schupp/iStockphoto, 23; Peeter Viisimaa/ iStockphoto, 24; Tom Rodriguez/Globe Photos, Inc., 27; Raymond Boyd/Getty Images, 37, 71, 97; Lauren Greenfield/ AP Images, 46; Ron Edmonds/AP Images, 49; Fitzroy Barrett/ Globe Photos, Inc., 51; EG/Globe Photos, Inc., 59; Justin Sutcliffe/AP Images, 61, 98 (top); Kimberly Butler/Getty Images, 62; Krusberg/IPOL/Globe Photos, Inc., 67; Robert Kalfus/AP Images, 69; Frank van den Bergh/iStockphoto, 72; Paul Skipper/AP Images, 74; Frank Wiese/AP Images, 77; Tom Rodriguez/Globe Photos, Inc., 79, 99 (top); Kelly Jordan/ Globe Photos, Inc., 85; Malcolm Payne/Getty Images, 87, 98 (bottom); Andrea Renault/Globe Photos, Inc., 91; Annette Brown/Getty Images, 93, 99 (bottom); Globe Photos, Inc., 95